The Gospel Car

Stephen Hatcher

British Library Cataloguing in Publication Data.

A catalogue record for this book is available from the British Library

ISBN 978 0 86071 893 2

A Commissioned Publication Printed by
MOORLEYS
Print, Design & Publishing
info@moorleys.co.uk • www.moorleys.co.uk

THE GOSPEL CAR

(Also known as a MISSION VAN)

Contents

Chapter 1: The Church Army on the Road

During the 20 years before World War One, the biggest operator of Gospel Cars was the Church Army. Under the dynamic leadership of Wilson Carlile, the Church Army was the social conscience of the Church of England in action. To put it simply: it was like the Salvation Army but coming from within the Church of England. Moreover, Wilson Carlile showed not just compassion but considerable diversity, when reaching out to the poor, the lost and the lonely of late Victorian and Edwardian society.

Having taken holy orders Wilson Carlile engaged in a wide range of ministry, from magic lantern shows for ruffians who arrived to 'play up' but sometimes stayed to be 'captivated and won', to the homeless on the Thames Embankment, to the visitation of those in prison, the barrack room and on the street. Wherever human beings were without human dignity as Children of God, there the Church Army aimed to be.

A particularly successful work was undertaken during those 'turn of the century' years with the Gospel Car or the Mission Van as the Church Army preferred to call it. In fact, there is perhaps a subtle class distinction here. While the Wesleyans had *Gospel Cars*, the Church Army and the Primitive Methodists had *Mission Vans*.

The idea of using these vans occurred to Mr Carlile in 1892. He was much attached to the reports of the system of the preaching friars in the 13th Century and the horseback journeys of John Wesley in the 18th Century. Wilson Carlile did not originate the idea of travelling preachers' vans but he developed the work to such an extent that by 1904, there were 66 such vans on the road under the direction of the Church Army, more than all the other operators put together.

If any young man felt a call to the Church because he thought that it would be any easy life, he was quickly disillusioned on the Mission Van. The crew (two or often three were in the van) rose at 6am, dressing in turn because of limited space. The stove needed cleaning and lighting, and water needed fetching. Bible reading and prayer would follow, or, if the van was near to the parish church, a short walk for Holy Communion was also taken, with a rapid return for breakfast. After a substantial Bible study the brothers would venture out visiting and bookselling. Lunch was likely to be meat and potatoes with more visiting in the afternoon.

All those whom they met, wherever and however they were met, would be invited back for a big meeting to be held around the van in the evening when the labourer's work was done. With careful time management, supper, prayers and bed all followed just before 11.00 pm.

It was heroic work and shared with other denominations. The Wesleyans, led by Thomas Champness, were the next largest group. Their story will be told in the next two chapters.

The Church Army van and officers with a bicycle are on the road to a new destination.

Is this a good location?

Or is this site better?

This is the place! It's near to a community but has plenty of space for a crowd to gather.

With the aid of the motorbike, even more people will hear the news of our arrival!

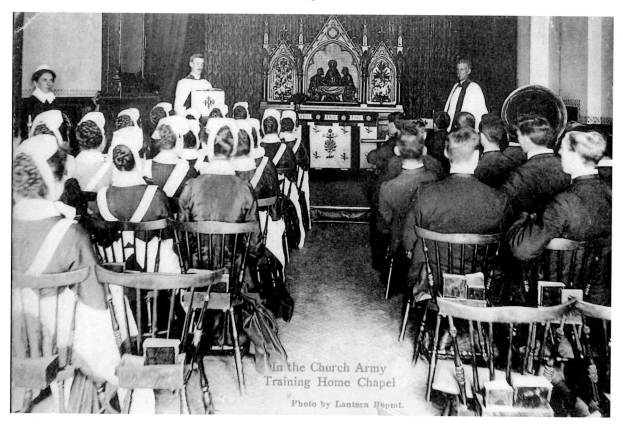

Just remember the training that we received before we set out!

*Don't be afraid to consult with colleagues when need arises -
another team are working not far away!*

Note the different design of this van, including a minimal platform and no rail at the front. Children, of course, would find the van an immense attraction.

The call was to tough urban locations - the Wakefield area!

The van also moved to village sites. Note that the design of this van is such that it does not have a front platform at all and has a side door to the interior of the van.

Sometimes the van would work closely with the local Church - in this instance at Llandaff.

Sometimes the support of that Church was quite magnificent!

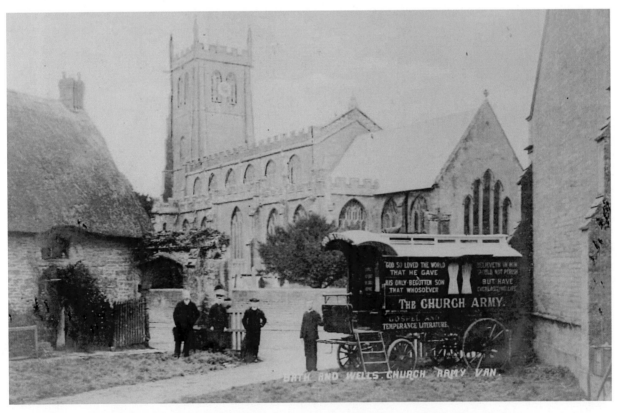

*Here is a picture of the Bath and Wells Church Army Mission Van -
no-one could possibly doubt the strong 'link' between Van and Church.*

The Church Army did not hesitate to move with the times.
They made the transition from the horse to the internal combustion engine
as is illustrated by this Motor Van used in Bradford 1925-6.

During the period between World War I and World War II, the Church Army
claimed that 64 Mission Vans were at work in Great Britain and Ireland.
This Van is pictured outside St Peter's Episcopal Church, Townsend Place, Kirkcaldy.

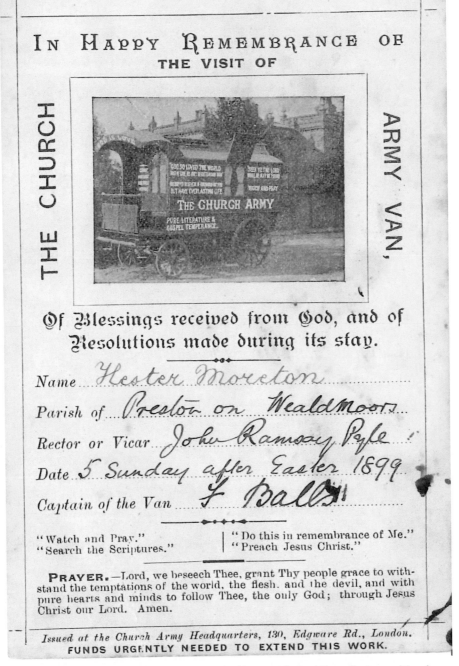

IN HAPPY REMEMBRANCE OF
THE VISIT OF

THE CHURCH

ARMY VAN,

THE CHURCH ARMY

PURE LITERATURE &
GOSPEL TEMPERANCE.

Of Blessings received from God, and of
Resolutions made during its stay.

Name *Hester Moreton*

Parish of *Preston on WealdMoors*

Rector or Vicar *John Ramsay Pyle*

Date *5 Sunday after Easter 1899*

Captain of the Van *F Balls*

"Watch and Pray."   "Do this in remembrance of Me."
"Search the Scriptures."   "Preach Jesus Christ."

PRAYER.—Lord, we beseech Thee, grant Thy people grace to withstand the temptations of the world, the flesh, and the devil, and with pure hearts and minds to follow Thee, the only God; through Jesus Christ our Lord. Amen.

Issued at the Church Army Headquarters, 130, Edgware Rd., London.
FUNDS URGENTLY NEEDED TO EXTEND THIS WORK.

'In Happy Remembrance of the Visit of the Church Army Van'.

Chapter 2: The Life of Owd Mo

During the closing years of the 19th Century, the Wesleyan 'trainer of evangelists' Thomas Champness worked with some extremely unlikely people. One such was Owd Mo (Moses Welsby). All the Methodist groups had grown in 'respectability' to some extent during the 19th Century, but equally there were still those in all parts of Methodism who remembered the first calling to 'seek and save the lost'. Among the 'rescued' was Owd Mo, who wrote:

You know the devil is an old sweater. You work for him long hours, and he pays you with sore bones, a starving family, a ruined character, a blighted life, an empty cupboard and hell! After doing all you can for him! (Specific reference to gambling and alcohol is made) Man turn to God, and live! Why will ye die? Never mind how dark you are, Christ will give you light. And where there is light there is liberty.

The local Wesleyan itinerants were 'messengers of light' to Owd Mo and his fellow colliers during the early days when he still struggled violently with his former addictions. For instance the circuit superintendent, the Rev Thomas Wilkes, gave every Friday night to meet with 30 or 40 colliers to give Bible lessons. Further the Revs Benjamin Dodd and Arthur Westcombe conveyed a joy from within as they were always willing to take a dirty hand and they were also willing to preach in the streets. Owd Mo was transformed and it wasn't long before he took a chair with a good sound bottom and he was launched as a preacher outside the very public house where he had been such a former regular customer.

Through Mr Samuel Chadwick (as he was then) working as a lay evangelist at Stacksteads, Owd Mo was introduced to the 'Joyful News Mission'. There at the Mission he of course met the Rev Thomas Champness, who clearly saw the potential of this recent convert. For the next few months, as Owd Mo put it himself, 'wet or dry I was by his side'. The decisions were then made to: 'train' Owd Mo, send him to London, and also offer a 'caravan'.

On August 5 1887, Owd Mo made his first acquaintance with the Gospel Car (a former gypsy caravan purchased for £20 known as a Joyful News 'Ark', and with Drummer the horse). 'Poor Old Drummer, very willing but slow' was the way that Owd Mo summed up the progress of his horse. However, Owd Mo was not just travelling from one village to the next - but from county to county, and moving from Banbury via Grimsbury, Quinton, Pershore, Himbleton, Kidderminster, Stourport, Walsall, Bilston, Brownhills, Ashton and Oldham and preaching all the way, until finally coming to Rochdale and the Joyful News HQ. There in the care of Mrs Champness the horse was given two days rest and in due course 'full retirement'. There is no report of any rest taken by Old Mo.

Back on the road and reaching Farnworth, Owd Mo went to the market inspector to ask for a stand for his Bible Van. The inspector agreed and indicated that there would be no charge. Was this just because it was a good cause, or did the inspector know more about the life of the man who was making the request than he let on? Owd Mo himself knew the significance of the site: 'Friends this was the spot where I had many a time been stripped for a fight, and where I used to sing the drunkard's song'.

But now the words of the song had been transformed as had the life of the preacher. Owd Mo would write: 'My heart was full of love for my old mates, with tears I prayed to God for help. That evening the men that I had gambled with and been at the ale-bench with, and others of my neighbours, spent over nine pounds for Bibles and good books'.

Owd Mo continued his caravan mission for eight years at 'full-steam' but then had to recognise that he was 'a broken man'. However he did not blame his toil as a preacher for the weakened body, rather he saw his worsening state as due to wasted years of misspent youth on the ale-bench and its associated activities. 'After much prayer and sorrow of heart I had to say to Mr Champness that I must give up the van work, as I could no longer stand it.' Thomas Champness wisely agreed and the way was opened for younger men.

Why was Owd Mo so successful? What was his secret? Yes it was the work of God, but why this particular servant? Owd Mo himself was the other half of the answer:

In one of my missions I went one day into 20 homes where there was little food and the children naked; a great many of the fathers had to leave the village and go elsewhere to seek work, as the collieries were flooded and the ironworks stopped. I could not get down on my knees to pray for these dear children. I went off to the grocer with a few shillings of my own, spent up, distributed it as well as was possible as far as it would go, and then I prayed in their homes.

Chapter 3: Thomas Champness: A Joyful Newspaper, a Joyful News Wagon, a Joyful News Training College

Thomas Champness.

Thomas Champness was a remarkable man who brought a three-fold overall strategy to Gospel proclamation during the last two decades of the nineteenth century and into the early years of the twentieth century also.

He had grown up in poverty. His father had tramped from town to town in search of work, and even when they settled, the Champness family sat in the free seats at the Manchester George Street Wesleyan Chapel because they could not afford to 'rent a pew'.

Selected for the Wesleyan ministry and with just two weeks training, Thomas Champness was sent to the West Coast of Africa in 1857 - 'the white man's grave' as it was known of Sierra Leone. Inevitably, he fell victim of the fever, however, miraculously he survived and returned home, while many others didn't. He had grown up in poverty, he had faced death, and with a deep faith that had sustained him until now, he turned to proclaim the Gospel back in the UK.

Of course, he nourished his soul in a way that was in line with the historic Christian faith of personal and corporate devotion. Of course, he put himself where the 'lost souls' were to be found - on the streets. Of course, he offered hope, whether in the form of a hot meal or Christian fellowship. However, the remarkable achievements of Thomas Champness were due also to the development of a threefold strategy:

A Joyful Newspaper: A cheaply produced popular paper distributed on the street achieved 'conversation' and 'converts'.

A Joyful News Wagon: A small mobile home with a horse to move it offered flexibility of movement and a bed for the night for the preacher or preachers when a new destination was reached.

A Joyful News Training College: This enabled basic instruction to be given not just to one at a time, but to a whole team of preachers.

The strategy of Thomas Champness worked well in enabling the Wesleyan Methodists to become the second biggest operator of travelling evangelists with mission vans in the field - only the Church Army having a larger number.

Having decided what to do, Thomas Champness then moved quickly to bring these three inter-related strategies into play. Telling the 'Champness story' Josiah Mee, one of the biographers of Champness put it like this:

It was not long after the start of the paper that Mr Champness and I went to the dedication and opening service of the first mission car we had seen. Mr Carr, of the York Wesley Circuit had built it. Most of the money had been found by some Quaker ladies of that city. The new book-van, as it was also called, had been taken to Selby, and there in the market-place we found it. With singing and prayer and short Gospel addresses, the new enterprise was commenced, and an evening meeting held in a small hall.

The following day journeying back to Lancashire Mr Champness declared with great emphasis and confidence to Josiah Mee 'We must have one of those'. And he did - big style.

The work grew at a rapid pace, with more and more Gospel Car preachers being trained, and this in turn meant that greatly enlarged premises were required. Castleton Hall was purchased, providing 'space' for those at the beginning of their ministry, and also for those needing a break from the ongoing work. If Moses Welsby and the other colporteurs needed to bring home the vans for a time, Castleton Hall now provided stables and yards that were available for cover, maintenance and repair.

What was the reason for his considerable success? Simply, Thomas Champness was a man of God, and because of that he was a man of the people. On one occasion he said:

Don't you say I'm a Socialist! I am merely giving you some Old Testament ideas. 'Bring back the land to the people.' As it was said of his Lord: 'The common people heard him gladly'
(Luke 4 v.15).

Moses Welsby - Owd Mo.

It is claimed that this is Gospel Car No. 5 'Peace' which travelled during 1905-07 in the Nottingham - Derby area.

There is no doubt that this is Ebenezer. Note that two of the preachers have bikes.

This Gospel Car was known as 'Rev Thomas Cook's Home Mission Car Number 16'.

Gospel Car Number 24 was known as Peniel, a name which recalled the name of the place where Jacob 'strove with God' (Genesis 32 vv.22-32).

*The smartest appearance was required for this preacher in Oxfordshire
(the card has a Watlington postmark) - but this might not be quite the
right image if the Gospel Car was going to the beach!*

Quite a crowd!

Chapter 4: Primitive Methodists in Lincolnshire

During the closing years of the 19th Century, the idea of a Primitive Methodist Mission Van for the villages of Lincolnshire gathered momentum. After some two and a half years of thinking and planning, an order was placed in May 1901 with Messrs. Buckingham of Birmingham, and three months later the van was delivered.

The cost of this portable 'church, manse, pulpit and book-stall' combined with furniture and a stock of books was £130. However at the point of the purchase of the 'the big idea', the faith that lay behind it was far more evident than the size of the bank balance. Just £40 was in hand, £90 was still to be found; however there was also a Dr J C Wright JP as treasurer of the fund now enthusiastically leading the fundraising programme.

Dr Wright was clearly a leading Primitive Methodist layman in the Lincolnshire District, with the distinction within society of being both a 'doctor' and a JP. Yet he had also made his spiritual home among the humble rural Primitive Methodists of Lincolnshire.

Such identification had happened elsewhere within Primitive Methodism, but it did not happen often! For instance, Squire Shafto of Bavington Hall, Northumberland, was another example of someone with social standing who warmly embraced Primitive Methodism. Robert Ingram Shafto, notwithstanding his long pedigree was on the Primitive Methodist class list of members. There was nothing that he liked better than having Primitive Methodists on his estate and round his table. 'He delighted to join enthusiastically in a rousing camp meeting with as much zest as a shepherd or a ploughman.'

The *Christian Messenger* in December 1901 reported as follows:

By visiting the several circuits in the District, and personally canvassing the subscriptions, he (Dr Wright) succeeded in raising the entire amount. When the liabilities of the capital account were discharged there was a small balance to transfer to the current account. In this successful enterprise Dr Wright was ably seconded by the ministers and laymen of the respective circuits, and not least by the Rev. J Keighley, the secretary of the missionary affairs for the District. At Dr Wright's request, Victoria, Countess of Yarborough, very kindly loaned to the van mission a small harmonium, which is of great service to the missioners.

The two first missioners appointed were from Scotland, and products of impact of Primitive Methodism in Blantyre, Lanarkshire and the ministry of the Rev F J Sainty. Mr Peter Bryce and Mr William Muir as Scots were well-educated, well-spoken, and had both left lucrative positions for the now varied and far less secure itinerant life of evangelistic preaching, conducting children's missions, advocating temperance, selling cheap literature and visiting from house to house.

It was recognised that the villages of Lincolnshire had suffered from rural de-population during the last quarter of the 19th Century. A drift to the towns of those who were perhaps most ambitious and able in recent years had impacted upon those within the rural society that was left. Thus the rural Mission Van made a very positive statement.

With reference to the national position the *Christian Messenger* report concluded with these words:

The work of the Van Mission is succeeding. The Wesleyans have fifteen Missions Cars, and are about to build five more. In the report for their work for the past year it is stated that: 'through the joint agency of the Colporteur, over twelve hundred pounds worth of books have been sold, and over five thousand persons have decided for God, most of whom have joined that Church'.

The future looked extremely promising. The Mission Van or Gospel Car was to be an extremely useful tool in the evangelisation of this land. Of course, at that point none of them saw the tragedy ahead of World War One. Not only would it 'change everything' in regard to 'method', it would offer the biggest challenge to 'faith' experienced within so-called civilized society thus far!

Children gather by the Gospel Car adjacent to Edlington Colliery, near Doncaster.

Two smartly dressed preachers with their Mission Van are located in what appears to be a 'middle-class area' - note the double fronted house and the passing horse and trap. What would be an open platform area on other Primitive Methodist Vans is also totally enclosed.

This preacher is also smartly dressed and elegantly positioned with one foot on the wheel and the other foot on a step to the platform. The picture was taken by Thatcher and Son, photographers from the ancient town of Tadley, Hampshire.
This is presumably where the Gospel Car was working.

The preacher has achieved some success and obtained an entree into Society. Here he is demonstrating a serious sense of purpose with a pulpit-sized bible open on the table in front of him. If that is vegetation on a trellis behind him - he could even still be speaking in the open air!

This group of supporters are probably standing on either side of the Mission Van preacher who is positioned slightly to the left of centre on this picture. The card has 'Mr Mansell' written on the reverse side - perhaps he was the preacher. The location is not known.

Chapter 5: The Salvation Army: The Gospel and Glory

During 1906, a series of articles appeared in the newspaper 'The Daily Graphic' suggesting that the Salvation Army was neither entirely sound in relation to spiritual matters, nor in relation to organisational or financial matters. Specifically, the articles cast doubt on the position of the 'Army' as a body engaged with rescue work of those in the gutter. This may have been true once, but it was argued by the 'Graphic' that 'the Army is now rather more concerned with building its own organisation and its own glory'.

The paper put it like this: 'During the last few years the Army has become to its great undoing, almost fashionable. Nothing, as everyone knows, is as beneficial to a new sect as persecution. In the days of its lusty youth, the Salvation Army had enough and to spare. But of late years a reaction has set in its favour. Great towns presented the freedom of their cities to General Booth, and it was held up as a philanthropic institution for the saving of submerged souls, run on the most business-like principles'.

His Majesty King Edward VII had set his seal on the General and the Army by receiving him in 1904 at Buckingham Palace. 'You are doing a great work General Booth, the success of which I regard with great importance to my Empire,' the king hastened to say.

However the 'Graphic' writer argued that the constant glorification of General William Booth - from royalty to those who flocked on the streets with applause wherever he ventured - was totally out of proportion. The Army had allowed success to go to its head and had taken its eye off the ball.

Indeed the national tours by the General in his glorious 'Gospel Car' were now also seen by some as part of the problem of that glorification.

The first motor campaign was from Penzance to Aberdeen, occupying 29 days and covering 1,224 miles. Without a doubt he delighted in this campaign.

'We are on the cars,' he wrote. 'All along the route we have ever been saying: There are the people; there is the blessed flag. They are at the windows, or on the roadside; in the street, everywhere. Hallelujah!'

In fact, the journey was marked with constant repetition of such scenes. 'And the dear, waiting, watching crowds, as they have seen us approach have said: Look they are coming!' Then: 'They are racing down the hill, along the valley. There are the flags! They are here! That is the General! Hurrah! Hallelujah!'

Despite the mud and the wet, despite the fact that he was now 75 years of age, the General disembarked and proceeded to address yet another rejoicing crowd that day.

So for whose benefit was this glorious Gospel Car being used? Was it for the Gospel of God, or for the glorification of the General?

In drawing a conclusion, the reader is asked to note two vital facts: William Booth and the Salvation Army had endured ridicule, persecution and at times imprisonment for very many years. Christian disciples do not always come to 'glory' in this life, however if (as in this case) the value of the work later comes to be recognised by 'king and people' then why should these worthy servants themselves also not rejoice?

The scope of the newly invented limousine was vastly superior to that of the horse-drawn Gospel Car. William Booth saw a potential that others did not see. So if he saw the potential and used the opportunity to preach more times to more different crowds than would have been possible with an earlier horse drawn cart - then isn't that also an occasion to rejoice?

The General is well 'wrapped up', and ready to take his seat (or stand) in the open top car.

*The white-bearded and capped General stands in the rear of the open top car
to begin his journey to meet the welcoming crowd.*

General Booth is on tour.

Chapter 6: Caravan Mission: Others in the Field

The 1920s was not a decade when Gospel Cars were conspicuous by their presence among rural or urban communities. World War One had taken many of the best young men and, for those who returned, their native land was a land where little work was to be found.

The perspectives of the Christian Church about what was needed and what was relevant in the 1920s had also changed. For instance, Southlands Wesleyan Church, Bishopthorpe Road, in York decided to respond by building a 'Thanksgiving Hall'. This was a building expressing thankfulness that the war was over, expressing thankfulness that some had returned, but also expressing deep regret that the 'land fit for heroes' was one in which there wasn't even work for those heroes to do.

However it would be some recognition from the Christian Church if they could at least spend some time together around a snooker table within the wholesome atmosphere of the 'Thanksgiving Hall', rather than in the doubtful atmosphere of the public house. For many churches, the 1920s was a time of 'practical Christianity' and not a time for 'Hot Gospel' Mission Vans.

However, during the first three decades of the 20th Century there were still a small number of Mission Vans in operation - some by other organisations. The Unitarians had at least one such Van.

Unitarian Mission Van before meeting time.

The Church Missionary Society also had at least two such Vans.

'God Willing' Mr Hudson Jermy offered Gospel services in the Clitheroe area.

Sometimes it appears that the preachers were intent on frightening the public into the faith.

It was far more positive to show the friendly face of the local vicar and a friendly congregation at St Mary and All Angels the Figheldean parish church in 1911 as they paraded with the Gospel Car.

Those who could not afford a Gospel Car could perhaps afford a Gospel Bicycle.
Or perhaps they did have a Gospel Car and that vehicle had dropped off two bicycles and one harmonium to work this particular 'patch' while the Gospel Car had moved on elsewhere. There is just so much that we may never ever fully know!

Here are two further Gospel Cars and each with the slogan 'God is Love'. Nothing can be added about this all male group other than that which can be deduced from the picture.

The Princess Mary Caravan, pictured, was a sizeable vehicle working for the Girls Friendly Society and showing here five of the workers. The Society was established in 1875 and is one of the oldest registered charities to support girls and young women in England and Wales.

Over in America, a Gospel Car more the size of a small bus was in use. It would travel from city to city holding open-air Gospel Meetings every evening. The Fulton Gospel Auto was 23 feet long, 10 feet high and 8 feet wide. It was based at Harrisburg, Pennsylvania and available to work with churches by prior arrangement.

NEW YORK'S TRAVELLING CHURCH.
The Rev. Brandford Clarke, a New York clergyman, standing beside the miniature church mounted on a motor chassis from which he preaches as he travels from place to place. This travelling church contains, among other things, a small organ.

Here also is New York's Travelling Church.

This is a Van offering 'Peace'. The word can be seen in fairly large letters on the door of the Gospel Car. The three storey buildings behind the Gospel Car and the tree to the left of the picture suggest that this Gospel Car was in a public place, and possibly a market square. A congregation cannot be seen in the picture, however it is quite possible that a congregation was present and the two leaders on the platform were in progress of taking a service. One leader is playing the small organ, while the other is speaking or singing. This Gospel Car is something of a mystery because neither on the image of the Gospel Car nor on the card on which it is printed is there any reference to denomination, location or occasion!

Another newcomer to the field was the Manchester City Mission. During the years 1925 and 1926, the Manchester City Mission put three of these Cars on the road with a slight change of title. The Gospel Car or Mission Van of the Methodists and Anglicans had now become 'The Gospel Caravan Mission' of this independent, theologically conservative, non-sectarian mission, as they described themselves.

Caravan No 1 was dedicated on Saturday 2 May 1925 and set off on an eight month tour of the villages of Cheshire and the Salford Dockland. The following year, the caravan included Derbyshire as well. Caravan No 2, known as the J D Brocklehurst Memorial Caravan, travelled around the coal mines and cotton mills of industrial Lancashire. Caravan No 3 joined the activity from Monday 23 August 1926.

The pattern of life for the missioners was very similar to that already encountered when looking at other churches with vans in the earlier decades:

Two missioners were in charge of each caravan and made it their bedroom at night. It was their kitchen, study, prayer room and inquiry room by day; and platform for the proclamation of the Evangel in the evening.

Local clergy and ministers were contacted on arrival of the caravan in their community and cooperation was sought for the 14 day mission. The village was 'consecutively visited' with the day concluding with a two to three hour special service around the van in the evening. It was believed that the results were 'truly wonderful'.

However, the Methodists had not totally relinquished this field. They moved to caravans as well and the work of the Wesley Deaconess Caravan Mission is still within living memory. At Mow Cop Chapel, Staffordshire, there are still those who remember thankfully the Wesley Deaconess Mission of their childhood or youth.

Further, with the assistance of J Arthur Rank money channelled through Methodist Home Missions in the late 1940s, the present writer can remember a Mobile Cinema Van coming to a bomb site near to where he lived and with internal projection showing films on the rear of the van.

It is also clearly remembered that a good crowd of the young gathered round. These were the days, of course, before television was at all widespread, and this visit to the Mobile Cinema Van was perhaps the visit to the 'pictures' for some of those who gathered, that they had not been able to afford that week - in those days of considerable austerity.

The mobile cinema van offered 'pictures' on the bomb sites in the years immediately after WW2; however it was also available for a second activity on the streets. The two young and very friendly Methodist ministers were on the lookout for 'memories' and 'opinions' from those who were passing by. This was quite different from preaching 'at them'! This was asking them about what they thought. It was not, for the moment at any rate, telling them what the church wanted them to hear.

Deaconesses at Mow Cop.

In the picture, the Rev Cyril Blount and the Rev Brian Webb are shown to be using a tape recorder and microphone to engage with those who were passing and who were willing to express their opinions. Those taking part were told that the recording would be played back in church on Sunday to the congregation. The passing public as participants were warmly invited to be there to hear it.

The Methodist Church Home Mission Department is using a tape recorder on the street.

During the early 1960s, again under the direction of the Home Mission Department, a film often replaced the sermon in an otherwise 'normal' Sunday service in a Methodist Church. Congregations often grew to two or three times their normal size. Was it successful in the longer term or not? Who knows! At least the Methodist Church was trying really hard to do *something*!

So what is the calling to the Methodist Church and other Churches today: is it to *caravans, snooker tables* or *what*? Whatever else happens, that is a question that must never be allowed to go away!

Chapter 7: A Car-Church for Soldiers at War

The picture of the Gospel Car within the context of war shows a 'car-church', as it was described for German soldiers, in the field during World War One. It appeared in the 'Illustrated War News' dated 3 February 1915. The accompanying text informs the reader that the Cardinal Archbishop of Cologne had given 'a singularly practical illustration of the resourcefulness as well as the anxiety of the Church in the administration of the consolations of religion to soldiers on active service'. His Eminence the Archbishop himself had enabled the funding to be made available for the building of this 'church on wheels'.

This Gospel Car had been constructed to be about the size of an ambulance van. It was painted grey and bore a conspicuous red cross on the two sides. The altar was specially constructed to fit the space across the van from side to side, behind the rear wheels and right at the back of the van. With an altar facing backwards at the rear of the vehicle, it was perfectly placed for a congregation who would sit on the ground behind the Gospel Car under the shelter or shade of a tarpaulin if that should be needed - depending on the weather and temperature.

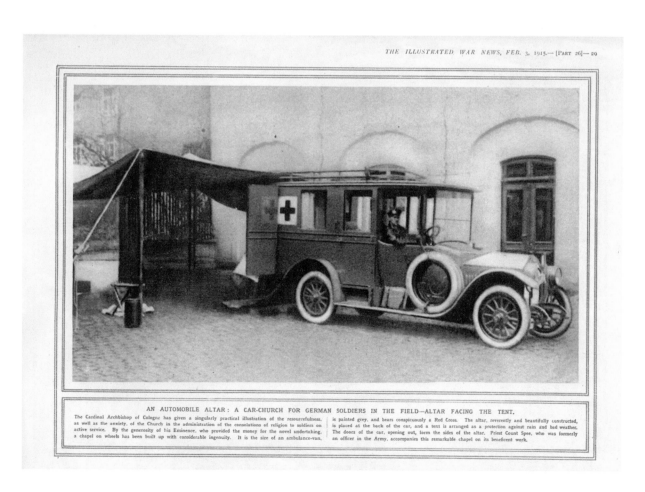

The picture shows this 'tent like' structure with a pole keeping the roof of the 'tent' above where the German soldiers could be seated. The reader is also informed that priest Count Spee, formerly an Army officer, 'accompanied this remarkable chapel in its beneficent work'.

On the British side, a 'Mobile Motor Church' was adapted from a heavy lorry and commissioned for World War Two. It was featured in the 'Illustrated London News' on 9 September 1944. In order to facilitate church services for British troops in the field, a number of mobile churches had indeed been provided by public subscription and this was one of them. On 25 July, the Archbishop of Canterbury had dedicated two of them - to St George and St Paul, to help the Royal Army Chaplains Department meet the spiritual needs of the troops in the Twenty-First Army Group on the continent.

The first of these new churches on wheels to reach France was utilised for service at General Montgomery's headquarters on Sunday 27 August 1944.

To us today, there is something quite incongruous about two allegedly Christian nations engaged in armed conflict with each other. The presence of a mobile church on both sides heavily underlines that point. However, there is a positive point: Amidst even 'war' the Christian Church was there. In the midst of the troops engaged in armed conflict to the death - the Gospel Car was there. That is a positive!

A MOBILE CHURCH : A service is conducted while the congregation takes tea at the church canteen.
The new mobile church, the first of its kind in Britain, has been arranged by the London Embankment Mission. It is stationed at Temple Place and services are being held four times a week. The vehicle used has two compartments; one forms the church with seats for twelve people; the other is the canteen and is fitted with a plastic and chromium sink. It weighs 2½ tons; is 23 ft. long; 10 ft. high and 8 ft. wide

A mobile church with canteen in action!

Chapter 8: Caravan Mission during the 20th and 21st Century

A picture has been painted in earlier chapters of activity that reaches back to the late 19th Century with the Wesleyans, Primitive Methodists and Church Army putting preachers on the road in many a horse-drawn wagon. Those years before World War 1 witnessed Gospel Car/ Mission Van activity at its peak. A picture has also been painted of continuing activity during the 20th Century, but at a much reduced pace with the Manchester City Mission coming onto the scene in the 1920s. However the Methodist Church re-joined the ranks of those with 'vans' in a significant way with the use of Wesley Deaconess Caravan Missions in the years immediately after World War 2. This next section of the story begins with a Caravan Ministry at Mow Cop. It is recalled that the 1807 camp meeting was held at Mow Cop on the very site where the present chapel now stands and this fact made Mow Cop a very appropriate place for a new form of flexible mission.

In the early 1950s Sister Beth Bridges who was from Somerset and Sister Margaret Horne who was from Sheffield were the two missioners who arrived with a caravan at Mow Cop - and in which they lived for the next 2-3 weeks.

Deaconesses at Mow Cop.

They were extremely active running a regular *Sunshine Corner* for children, taking weeknight and Sunday services for adults and undertaking a large amount of 'house to house' visiting. Appeals for decisions were regularly made and people responded. There is no doubt that there was a real benefit for the Mow Cop Chapel - some who attend that chapel today were led to find God in a far more real way during the mission than they had even done before. This is an occasion for thankfulness.

However, in terms of 'numbers' and the response of those who subsequently became 'Church leaders', the Pentecostal movement was the main beneficiary. In due course Mow Cop itself would have a Pentecostal Church and the roots for this would go right back to the deaconess mission. So while Methodists rejoice of course if they can help those who then join other traditions, there must also be a touch of sorrow that some of those who had found God on Methodist premises during the mission then felt that they needed to go elsewhere to continue to find him afterwards.

Deaconesses in caravans now belong to a period that is over sixty years ago, and research undertaken to date has revealed very little of this kind of activity within Methodism since. However, small 'chinks of light' have shown through. In the year 2002, Jane Pickering was a Deacon in the Methodist Church and stationed in the Louth Circuit. The circuit treasurer was a man who 'loved to use circuit money for mission'; the circuit superintendent the Rev David Newlove was in full support; and at Jane's prompting the circuit agreed that a circuit caravan should be purchased. When not 'on mission' it would be housed in the garden of one of the circuit manses.

Jane herself had experienced a Wesley Deaconess caravan mission when she was in her early teens, and this had impacted upon her. Many years later as a Deacon herself, which she had become at the age of forty, she wanted to engage in a way that she knew had some potential to help many others.

The Mission in which Jane and others engaged in 2002 was simple in comparison with what had gone before. No-one slept on the van overnight; the *missioners* were within easy reach of their own homes and they returned home for a good night's sleep. There was no public preaching either, most conversations were on a 'one to one' basis, with the inside of the van being used if there was the need for privacy. Sometimes of course the conversation was with a small group. The key was to go where there were plenty of people and engage in conversation with those who wished. It worked!

The sites where this was possible were as follows: the Mablethorpe Co-op car park, the North Somercotes caravan park, Cadwell Park in Louth, where motor bike racing took place, and in Saltfleet where it was possible to 'latch on to' a car boot sale.

Did the wider public at these sites want to stop and talk? Yes they did! Free tea and coffee was on offer, and most visitors obviously judged that a free hot drink was fair exchange for a few minutes talking about religion! It was so beautifully simple that almost any church should be able to do it.

After two years it was believed that most people within that area who could be contacted had been contacted. It was felt that a natural terminus had been reached, so the mission concluded. The caravan was sold, and the circuit got most of its money back. A positive welcoming face had been shown by the Christian Church to the community; people had been reached in a caring non-threatening way; and the overall conclusion was that great good had been done.

Chapter 9: Brave Attempts After the Gospel Car

Cliff College Trekkers continued the tradition of being a 'mobile church' during the 1940s and 1950s. It was hard going as well - the trekkers themselves took the place of the 'horse' while the Gospel Car itself became the truck for their baggage.

There was now no prospect of the shelter of a Gospel Car on route, nor the prospect of taking a ride for a while - with the horse doing the work. At night they would hopefully sleep by prior arrangement on the floor of a Sunday School building.

The trekkers set out from Cliff College.

By the 1960s, road traffic had increased substantially and it was believed that there was an increasing risk of accident during the course of making the journey. The prospect of a trek cart travelling at a maximum of four miles an hour round a 'blind bend' with constant traffic in both directions of the road became an 'accident waiting to happen' and thus an increasing nightmare. The step was therefore taken to use a mini-bus to move the trekkers.

The present writer recalls that during the year 1964-5 he travelled on a mini-bus journey from Cliff College to a Lincolnshire chapel which became a base for a few days. Then the journey continued on from there to Bridlington. For a few weeks the trekkers would engage daily with the passing public on the sea front. The activity that took place included a morning and evening service and work with children in the afternoon.

It was also difficult to gather a crowd. Very often when Harold Goodwin started to play his piano accordion and the trekkers started to sing the public would begin to gather. Unfortunately when the singing stopped and the preaching began the public started to move on! It was very difficult to gather and keep a crowd. However it could be done, Norman Smith a Cliff College Evangelist and the team leader could do it. He could gather a crowd and he could hold them. Frankly while most of the rest of us could 'gather a few' we could not 'hold' even them.

The trekkers themselves had come without any personal resources and would depend for their stay in Bridlington on the generosity of the congregation of the local Methodist Church. Using the Church as a base the trekkers would prepare and eat their meals on site and that was where they would sleep on a camp bed at night.

These pictures show some success of the Christian Church in the open air since late Victorian times:

The Gospel Car, a tent for a big evening meeting and a crowd of children.

The Church Army on the beach at Morecombe has gathered a modest audience.

With or without a Gospel Car it was still possible in Edwardian times to gather a substantial crowd for an Open Air Service in some parts of the country as at Douglas Head.

The Methodist Church Beach Services picture was taken in 1939 and reveals that the Methodists (including the minister) were engaged in regular open air witness at this time.

A series of articles about 'Gospel Cars' in the *Methodist Recorder* during late 2020 and early 2021 provoked further information from Dorothy Robinson about Gospel Car activity in more recent years. She reported as follows:

The 'Derbyshire Village Mission' was founded by a wealthy London businessman, Robert Scase, who had become fascinated with Derbyshire by studying water colour paintings that he had acquired of the area. He moved to East Lodge, Rowsley, where he became a local benefactor. There he also met a new Christian named John Williams and the two of them together set about inaugurating the *Derbyshire Village Mission*.

At first three wheeled horse-drawn vehicles toured the Derbyshire villages, but later more sophisticated caravans were introduced from the 1950s. The mission was inter-denominational and run by sisters who would contact local Church leaders in advance with a view to securing their support. The sisters offered to take services in the local churches as part of the bridge-building that they wished to achieve. Of course meetings were also held in and around the caravan and literature including printed bible study material was left while visiting houses. The last caravan mission was held in 2002/3 but some work continued without the caravan until 2020.

Chapter 10: Just an Interesting Story or a Challenge?

In addition to activity in Derbyshire reported by Dorothy Robinson there has still been, at the time of writing, other limited 'Gospel Car' mobile work which has taken place.

This has included 'Bus-Ny-Bannaghtyn' (Bus of Blessing) in the Isle of Man District taking hospitality, prayer and blessing to local communities. In the Lancashire District the 'Godly Play Bus' has visited schools to share Bible stories. While in the Sheffield District, a bus which first operated in Matlock was later used in Chesterfield to give hospitality and clothes to homeless and needy people.

Today at the Black Country Living Museum, visitors can view 'Grace', a replica of the historic Wesleyan Methodist Gospel Car which served in the Netherton area (not far from the museum) during the early years of the 20th Century. Without a doubt an impact is made upon those visitors today at the Museum as they step inside to view the compact area which served every purpose from domestic dwelling to small meeting room. There is a deep realisation that those who historically served on the Gospel Car clearly lived in a *very* different world from that of today. Their 'faith' must have meant everything to them. They were in fact 'heroic'.

This realisation of the achievements of the past through 'Mobile Mission' brings a very serious challenge to both the Christian Church and the visitor today!

Gospel Car currently at Black Country Living Museum.